✳ Contents

1. At home **5**
Cushion with star 6
Delicate screen 11
Antique-style photo frame 15
Pretty chair cover 16
Tablecloth with flowers 20
Patchwork quilt 23

2. For yourself **27**
Chic holdall 28
Shoulder bag 32
Embroidered shopping bag 36
Holdall with scalloped edging 40
Little bag 42
Pretty wallet 46

3. Celebrations **51**
Decorative wreath 53
Pretty wicker basket 54
Decorative candleholder 56
Place setting 58
Soft pompoms 60
Attractive cones 63

4. Little gifts **67**
Bag on a chain 68
Stole 71
Lavender pillows 73
Purse 77
Delicate gift bags 78
Beautiful boxes 84

Patterns **88**
Suppliers and Index **96**

KT-103-445

LLYFRGELLOEDD POWYS LIBRARIES

Linen & Lace

Chantal Sabatier

Simple-to-sew homestyle
charm using new and
vintage lace

Powys

37218 00513703 4

David and Charles
www.rucraft.co.uk

✳ Acknowledgements

I should like to say a big thank you to the editor for having accompanied me on this project which was so close to my heart. Thank you to Julie, Chloé and Marie for their support throughout and for the great care they took with their work. Thank you to Fabrice and Sonia for their magnificent photographs and for positioning my creations in such a pretty house!

To my husband and to my two daughters, for their support and their tremendous patience. To all the members of my family and to my friends, who encouraged us and offered their valuable support during this very busy time: writing a book whilst working, and moving house at the same time... it had to be done!

Thank you to all those who love sewing and who visit my blog regularly and leave me such encouraging messages. I've been blogging for over three years now and I never tire of hearing from you with your ever-increasing enthusiasm.

Look me up on my blog to hear about other adventures and to share ideas: www.cabanedeviolette.canalblog.com

A DAVID & CHARLES BOOK
© Éditions Mango Pratique 2010
Originally published in France as *Lin et Dentelles*

First published in the UK in 2011 by David & Charles

David & Charles is an imprint of F&W Media International, LTD
Brunel House, Forde Close, Newton Abbot, TQ12 4PU, UK

F&W Media International, LTD is a subsidiary of F+W Media, Inc.
4700 East Galbraith Road, Cincinnati, OH 45236

Chantal Sabatier has asserted her right to be identified as author of this work in accordance with the Copyright, Designs and Patents Act, 1988.

All rights reserved. No part of this publication may be reproduced, stored in a retrieval system, or transmitted, in any form or by any means, electronic or mechanical, by photocopying, recording or otherwise, without prior permission in writing from the publisher.

Readers are permitted to reproduce any of the patterns or designs in this book for their personal use and without the prior permission of the publisher. However the designs in this book are copyright and must not be reproduced for resale.

The authors and publisher have made every effort to ensure that all the instructions in the book are accurate and safe, and therefore cannot accept liability for any resulting injury, damage or loss to persons or property, however it may arise.

Names of manufacturers, products and product ranges are provided for the information of readers, with no intention to infringe copyright or trademarks.

A catalogue record for this book is available from the British Library.

ISBN-13: 978-1-4463-0067-1 paperback
ISBN-10: 1-4463-0067-6 paperback

Printed in China by RR Donnelley
for F&W Media International, LTD
Brunel House, Forde Close, Newton Abbot,
TQ12 4PU, UK

10 9 8 7 6 5 4 3 2 1

F+W Media publishes high quality books on a wide range of subjects. For more great ideas visit: **www.rucraft.co.uk**

✳ Metric conversion chart

TO CONVERT	TO	MULTIPLY BY
inches	centimeters	2.54
centimeters	inches	0.4
feet	centimeters	30.5
centimeters	feet	0.03
yards	meters	0.9
meters	yards	1.1

Measurements in this book have been given in metric – use this chart to convert the measurements to Imperial.

1. At home

Cushion with star

Delicate screen

Antique-style photo frame

Pretty chair cover

Tablecloth with flowers

Patchwork counterpane

✳ Cushion with star

Measurements: 50 x 50cm

26 x 52cm of unbleached medium-weight linen fabric · Fine white linen fabric: 52 x 52cm for the cushion back; two times 15 x 52cm for the front vertical strips; 18 x 18cm for the star; four times 4.5 x 50cm for the ties · 52cm of white cotton lace trim, 3.5cm wide · One cushion pad, 50 x 50cm

COVER

The star pattern is provided on page 94. Cut out one star from the small square of white linen. Attach the star to the centre of the unbleached linen by hand using blanket stitch (see page 15) or by machine using a small zigzag stitch. Cut the lace trim into two equal lengths. Attach them to the unbleached linen, by machine or by hand, above and below the star and 6cm from the edges.

Sew the two strips of white linen to the unbleached linen, right sides together, sewing 1cm from the edges, to make the patchwork on the front of the cushion.

Oversew the outside edges of the patchwork you have created, as well as those on the large square of white linen. Lay them on top of one another, right sides together. Sew three of the sides 1cm from the edges (leave the right side (facing you) of the finished cushion open). Cut the corners at an angle. Turn the cover right side out and press.

TIES

Press a turning of 1cm along the long edges of each of the strips for the ties. Fold the strips in half along the length, wrong sides together. Sew them along the length, folding one of the ends inside to give a neat finish.

Iron a 1cm hem along the open edge of the cushion cover. Pin the unfolded ends of the ties under the hem, placing them at equal distances from the seams and spacing them 15cm apart; make sure they are opposite each other at the front and the back. Sew the hem.

FINISHING TOUCHES

Press the cushion cover and insert the cushion pad.

✳ Delicate screen

Measurements: 1.20 x 1.60m

Scraps of natural fabric in shades of white and beige, in different weaves, a minimum of 26cm wide and in various lengths: lightweight linen fabrics; linen gauze; lightweight cotton fabrics; voiles; cheesecloth; embroidered linen or cotton (recycled from old linen or made yourself); broderie anglaise; lace fabric; Floral patchwork fabrics • Lace motifs • Scraps of lace trim • 14.60m of white cotton twill tape, 2cm wide • 1.25m of white linen trim, 2cm wide • Spray starch

PREPARATION

This screen is pieced together from five vertical strips of patchworked fabric and lace in various lengths. All the pieces are 26cm wide to form the 24cm wide strips that make up the finished screen.
Cut the pieces carefully. Some may be made from fabric and lace already joined together. Starch the cotton fabric (spray starch is not recommended for use on linen, unless you are used to it).
Sew the lace trimming horizontally or vertically on different pieces.

ATTACHING LACE MOTIFS

Pin the motif to the right side of the fabric. Attach by hand by sewing around the edge using a backstitch (see page 36). Using a pair of pointed scissors, remove the fabric at the back of the motif, as close to the sewing as possible (leave an allowance of around 3mm), taking care to lift it up to avoid cutting the lace.

ASSEMBLY

Join the pieces together one above the other, right sides together, alternating the fabrics and shades, to form five strips. Each strip ends at the bottom with a lace border (if not, leave an allowance to make a small hem once the strip is finished), and at the top with a piece of fabric without embroidery at least 6cm deep.
Carefully oversew the edges of the seam allowances; try as much as possible to prevent any imperfections from being seen through.

Carefully press the strips. Make sure that they are all the same width and that the edges are straight. Join them together, 1cm from the edges, wrong sides together (the seams are deliberately placed on the right side). Check that the seam allowances are even, then press them, laying them all in the same direction.
Pin cotton twill tape over each seam, ensuring that you cover the allowances, tucking it under itself at the bottom edge. Sew along each edge of tape with a fairly long stitch (at least 2.5mm). These seams should be very flat and neat. For each of the side edges, fold the cotton tape in half along its length, press the fold, fold the bottom end of tape under, then sew the tape to the side edge of the screen.
At the top of the screen, fold down and then sew a 1.5cm hem on the wrong side. Cut six 60cm lengths of cotton tape. Fold them in half to make ties. Pin the ties to the hem at the top of each vertical seam or hem. On the right side, hemstitch the linen trim to the upper edge so that it overlaps the screen a little; fold the ends to achieve a nice finish. Press the screen. Tie the ties to the desired pole.

{TIP}: TO CUT OUT PERFECT RIGHT-ANGLED PIECES, IT IS BEST TO USE A ROTARY CUTTER ON A CUTTING PAD.

✳ Antique-style photo frame

One frame for 18 x 24cm photo · One vintage postcard · 22 x 28cm of unbleached even weave linen · 18 x 24cm of wadding (batting) · Scraps of lace and ribbon · Small pieces of embroidery, motifs in lace, charms, buttons · Strong white sewing thread in silk or linen · 18 x 24cm of mountboard or card · Adhesive tape or craft tape for the frame · Repositionable spray adhesive

DECORATION

Topstitch around the edge of the linen to prevent it from fraying. Place the postcard in the centre of the linen. Use a pencil to lightly trace two lines 1cm apart, 5mm from the edges all around the postcard.

Spray adhesive onto the back of the postcard, then reposition it in the centre of the linen. Attach it using blanket stitch (see diagram opposite) using the pencil lines.

Sew the lace, ribbons, pieces of embroidery, charms and buttons around the card. Place the decorations however you wish, taking inspiration from the photographs.

ASSEMBLY

Attach the wadding (batting) to the mountboard using the spray adhesive. Place the linen on the wadding (batting) and cut the corners at an angle. Fold the edges of the linen over to the back of the mountboard, then stick them using adhesive or craft tape. Place the work in the frame and insert the back.

BLANKET STITCH

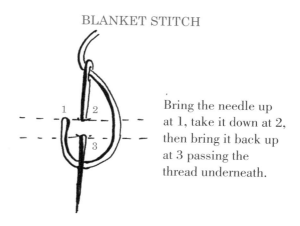

Bring the needle up at 1, take it down at 2, then bring it back up at 3 passing the thread underneath.

{TIP}: KEEP THE GLASS FROM THE FRAME, AS IT MAY BE USEFUL FOR OTHER PROJECTS.

✳ Pretty chair cover

Measurements: 40 x 40cm without the flounces

42 x 43cm of striped fabric in beige and ivory for the cushion top · 42 x 43cm of white linen fabric for the cushion back · 20 x 20cm of floral cotton fabric for the centre design · Three times 56 x 28cm of ivory linen gauze for the flounces · Four times 62 x 8cm of ivory cotton fabric for the ties · 1.2m of white broderie anglaise edging, 6cm wide (including a 2cm non-embroidered margin) · 1.2m of cotton piping cord · Two small sew-on press studs · One flat cushion pad, 40 x 40cm

TIES
Fold each of the strips for the ties in half along the length, wrong sides together. Press a 1cm turning along the long sides and at one of the ends (diagram 1). Sew close to the edge.

MAIN PIECES
Mark the centre of the striped cloth, bearing in mind that there is a 1cm seam allowance on the side and front edges, and 2cm for the hem at the back.

Press a 1cm turning to the wrong side all around the floral cotton. Centre this square on the right side of the striped cloth and attach it by machine using straight stitch.

Along the back edge of the cushion top, press a hem with a double fold of 1cm, then unfold. Repeat the operation on the white linen fabric.

①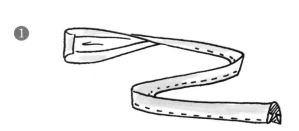

{TIP}: TO MAKE PERFECT FLOUNCES, ALLOW FOR MORE FABRIC THAN YOU THINK (AROUND 65 X 35CM PER FLOUNCE). PULL OUT SOME OF THE WEFT THREADS TO DETERMINE AN EVEN LINE FOR THE FLOUNCE, THEN CUT, FOLLOWING THAT LINE.

FLOUNCES

Fold each rectangle of linen gauze in half, right sides together (to obtain strips measuring 56 x 14cm).

Press them, checking that the edges are straight and well-aligned.

Sew the short sides 1cm from the edge, then oversew the edges.

Turn the flounces to the right side and press. Close the top, sewing 8mm from the edge. Make a second row of stitching at the same level using a very long running stitch, then gather to obtain a length of approx. 38cm.

EDGING

On the right side of the striped cloth, starting and ending 4cm from the back edge, pin the broderie anglaise edging around the three other sides, right sides together with the edging facing towards the inside, lightly gathering it in the corners (diagram 2). Sew it 2cm from the edges. Lay the piping cord in the seam allowance, turn the edging towards the outside and pin over the cord. Using the zipper foot on your sewing machine, sew the three sides as close as possible to the cord (diagram 3). Sew a small 5mm hem at each end of the edging for a neat finish (if necessary, cut off the excess fabric under the cord).

To prevent the edging from getting in the way during the following steps, lay it towards the centre and tack (baste).

ASSEMBLY

Place a linen flounce along one side edge of the cushion top, on the right side of the fabric, 4cm from the back edge and 1cm from the front edge. Sew 8mm from the edge. Proceed in the same way when attaching the flounce to the other side. Place the last flounce along the front edge, adjusting the gathers to allow a 1cm allowance on each side. Oversew around all the edges. Lay the three flounces towards the centre and tack (baste).

Oversew the edges of the white linen fabric. Place it on the striped cloth, right sides together, and stitch the three sides with flounces 5mm from the edges.

FINISHING TOUCHES

Turn the work right side out. Remove all the tacking (basting) threads, then turn the flounces and the edging to the outside.

Fold the hems along the back edges and press them. At each side, pin a tie beneath the hem of the striped cloth and another beneath the hem of the white linen, facing each other. Sew the hems, press them, then sew the two little press studs on the hems. Insert the cushion pad into the cushion cover.

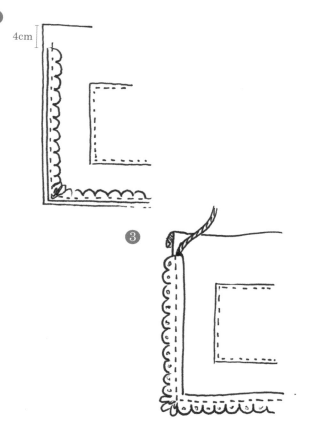

✳ Tablecloth with flowers

Measurements: 1.6 x 1.6m

For the tablecloth: 1.6 x 1.6m of unbleached lightweight linen • 6.5m of ivory lace trim, 2cm wide • 6.5m of white cotton twill tape, 2cm wide

For 12 flowers: 70 x 25cm of white cotton fabric • 70 x 25cm of unbleached linen fabric • 90 x 25cm transparent fabric (gauze or organdie) • 90 x 40cm iron-on interfacing • 12 small buttons in shades of white and beige • 12 small safety pins

TABLECLOTH

Cut the linen gauze following the weft threads to ensure that the edges are really straight. Cut the lace trim into four equal lengths. Pin them to the gauze 26cm from the edges. Sew them using a fairly long stitch to prevent them from puckering. Cut the excess trim level with the gauze. Fold the cotton twill tape in half along the length and press the fold. Sew the tape overlapping the gauze all around, so that the edges are covered.

FLOWERS

Reinforce the cotton and linen by bonding some iron-on interfacing to the reverse using an iron. With the help of the patterns provided on page 90, cut out six large petals and six small ones from the white cotton and from the unbleached linen; cut twelve small petals from the transparent fabric. For each flower, place two small petals on a large one, ending with a transparent one on top, then sew a button to the centre to hold it all together.

Note that not all the flowers are identical: alternate the order of the white petals and the unbleached ones, as well as the colour of the buttons.

FINISHING TOUCHES

Press the tablecloth. Spread the flowers over the overhanging area, attaching them with the small safety pins. That way, you can remove them when you wash your tablecloth.

For added impact spread the tablecloth over a larger white tablecloth, decorated in a similar fashion, as shown in the photo (opposite).

{TIP}: IT IS ADVISABLE TO BUY APPROX. 20CM MORE GAUZE THAN NEEDED SO THAT YOU CAN CUT A NICE NEAT SQUARE, WITH RIGHT ANGLES.

✳ Patchwork counterpane

Measurements: 1.3 x 1.3m

16 squares of lightweight fabric 30 x 30cm: four in beige striped fabric, four in unbleached linen fabric, four in floral cotton fabric, two in white linen fabric, two in pink striped cotton fabric · Two squares 20 x 20cm in white fabric, with an embroidered monogram approx. 8cm high · Approx. 40 x 40cm of cotton fabric with large flowers · Approx. 30 x 30cm of lace fabric with floral motifs · White cotton fabric 12cm wide for the edgings: two strips x 1.14m; two strips x 1.34m · 1.34 x 1.34m of white cotton fabric for the lining · 1.36 x 1.36m of wadding (batting) · 3.9m of lace trim with small roses, 2cm wide (see trim 1, page 25) · 1.2m of lace trim, 5cm wide (see trim 2, page 25) · 2.1m of lace trim with small roses (for the monograms) · Pair of compasses

CENTRE CIRCLES

Centre the compasses on the wrong side of each monogram, trace a circle 16cm in diameter, then cut out.

Attach each circle by machine to the centre of a square of unbleached linen. Using the photograph on page 25 for inspiration, attach a lace motif by hand, overlapping the linen and the monogram fabric, then finish edging the outer edge with some lace trim.

Cut some shapes following the outline of the motif from the cotton with large flowers. Attach one of them to the centre of each square of white linen, working by hand in blanket stitch (see diagram on page 15) or small, tight running stitch. Add some lace motifs.

Cut two circles 16cm in diameter from the cotton with large flowers. Attach them by machine to the centre of the two remaining squares of unbleached linen. Decorate and edge them as for the monograms.

{TIP}: TO MAKE SURE THE COUNTERPANE LOOKS NICE, WASH ALL THE FABRICS BEFORE JOINING THEM TOGETHER AND PRESS THEM WHILST STILL DAMP.

ASSEMBLY

Join the squares 1cm from the edges, right sides together (refer to the diagram on page 25 to see their layout). Attach the lace trims 1 and 2 by machine, arranging them as in the diagram. Join the two shortest strips of white fabric at the top and the bottom of the patchwork, 1cm from the edges, right sides together. Assemble the two remaining strips on the two other sides. Press your work. Attach some of lace trim 1, overlapping the patchwork and the long, vertical sides.

Spread out the lining, wrong side uppermost. Place the wadding (batting) on top, centring it. Tack (baste), radiating out from the centre, using long stitches up to approx. 2cm from the edges of the lining, then tack (baste) the outer edges. Cut the excess wadding (batting) level with the edges. Topstitch the outer edges using a large zigzag stitch.

Lay the lining and the patchwork right sides together. Sew together 2cm from the edges, leaving an opening about 40cm long.

Cut the corners at an angle. Turn the counterpane right side out and press. Fold the edges of the opening to the inside, then close them up using small stitches.

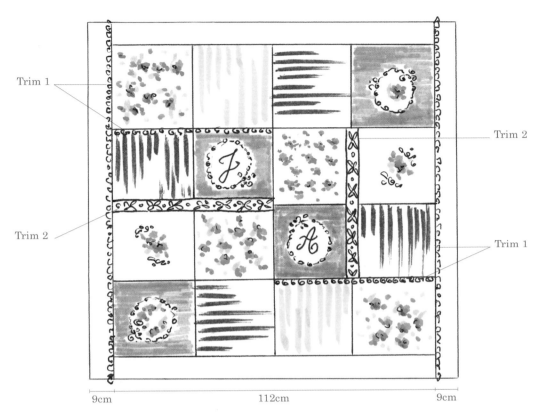

Trim 1

Trim 2

Trim 2

Trim 1

9cm 112cm 9cm

2. For yourself

Chic holdall

Shoulder bag

Embroidered shopping bag

Holdall with scalloped edging

Little bag

Pretty wallet

✳ Chic holdall

Measurements: 23 x 34cm without the handles

25 x 42cm of white medium-weight linen fabric • Medium-weight unbleached linen: two times 25 x 25cm for the holdall; two times 7 x 50cm for the handles • 25 x 88cm of white cotton fabric for the lining • 73cm of white lace trim, 2cm wide, for the holdall • 90cm of ivory lace trim, 1.2cm wide, for the handles • 8cm fine black ribbon • One embroidered monogram, approx. 6cm high • three buttons 1cm in diameter, for decoration • One pearlized button 1.5cm in diameter, for the fastening • 90cm of thick piping cord to reinforce the handles

For the flower: 1m of white satin tape, 2cm wide • Two lace trims, 1cm wide: 15cm white, 15cm ivory • 15cm black velvet ribbon, 5mm wide • Two silver metal charms

PLEATED FLOWER

Using an iron, press 6–7mm wide turnings along both long edges of the satin tape.
Sew right along the folds about 3mm from the edge. Roll up the tape in the shape of a flower, sewing the base by hand as you go along (diagram 1). Fold in the last centimetre and fix all the thicknesses firmly together at the base.

HANDLES

Fold each of the strips for the handles in half along the length, wrong sides together. Press a 1cm turning along the long sides. Place 45cm of piping cord into the fold and centre it. Sew the long, open side, starting and finishing 4cm from the ends. Turn under the ends by 5mm and pin. Attach the ivory lace along the outside of each handle 4cm from the ends.

1

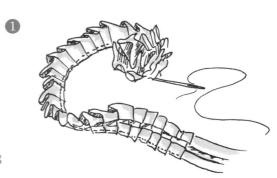

DECORATION

Sew the two squares of unbleached linen to either side of the white linen, right sides together, 1cm from the edges. Oversew the outer edges. Fold the piece in half from top to bottom, wrong sides together. Place it on the work surface, with the front side of the holdall uppermost. Attach 25cm of white lace trim to this side, overlapping the unbleached linen and the white linen. Attach the monogram 3cm above, centred widthways. Sew the flower firmly to the trim, attaching the two short lengths of lace and velvet ribbon, folded in half, underneath. Then attach the two charms under the flower. Sew the three decorative buttons onto the trim, spacing them approx. 3cm apart.

ASSEMBLY

Fold the linen piece in half from top to bottom, right sides together. Sew the two sides 1cm from the edges and oversew the edges.

Pinch in the two corners of the base, sew 5cm from the points, then cut the excess fabric 1cm from the stitching (diagram 2). Close up the lining and make the base, proceeding in the same way as for the linen.

Press all the seams, if possible on a sleeve-board.

Insert the lining into the linen, wrong sides together. At the top of the linen and at the top of the lining, fold down a 1cm hem towards the inside. Pin these hems to one another. At the centre back, pin the fine black ribbon folded into a loop between the two hems. Sew close to the top edge, then attach the remaining white lace trim to it.

FINISHING TOUCHES

Turn down the top of the holdall to the front by approx. 4cm. Sew on the pearlized button 1cm above the monogram. Pin on the handles at the same level, 3.5cm from the side seams. Sew them on firmly by hand using small stitches, opening out the fabric at the ends to make neat little triangles (diagram 3). Press the holdall, including the folds at the bottom.

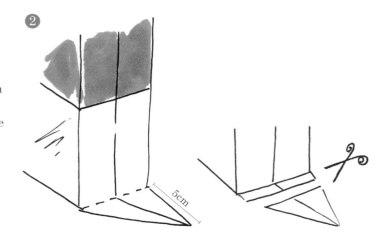

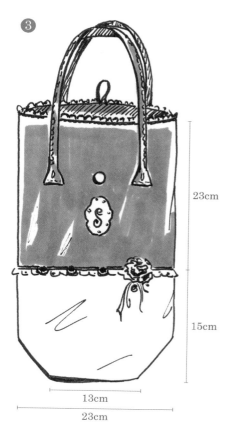

Front view (bottom not visible)

✳ Shoulder bag

Measurements: 35 x 32cm without the handles

Unbleached medium-weight linen fabric: two times 37 x 35cm for the bag; 20 x 20cm for the pocket • 37 x 68cm of lightweight cotton fabric for the lining • 22 x 12cm of embroidered tulle • 15cm of two lace trims in different cottons, 6cm wide • 37cm of ivory lace trim, 3cm wide • 20cm of fine white lace trim, for the pocket • 53cm of woven patterned ribbon, 1cm wide • 37cm brown satin ribbon, 2.5cm wide • 6cm of tape woven with the inscription 'made by hand', or similar • 70 x 40cm of iron-on interfacing • One pair of brown leather handles with holes for sewing, approx. 58cm long • Two patterned metal buttons: one 2cm in diameter, for the bag; the other a little smaller for the pocket • 11cm of elastic, 2.5cm wide • Strong white sewing thread in silk or linen

For the flower: 1m of ivory tape, 2cm wide • 15 x 15cm of thick white cotton fabric • 15 x 15cm of embroidered tulle • 15 x 15 of iron-on interfacing • 25cm of red velvet ribbon, 1cm wide

FLOWER

Make a folded flower using the tape, proceeding as explained on page 28. Reinforce the piece of white cotton by bonding the iron-on interfacing to the reverse using an iron. Using the pattern provided on page 90, cut out one large petal shape from the stiffened cotton and another from the embroidered tulle. Place the tulle petal onto the cotton one, join them at the centre with a few stitches, then sew the folded flower firmly on top.

TRIM

Cut 37cm of patterned ribbon, centre it on the satin ribbon, then sew together. Proceed carefully to get a neat result: sew close to each edge using a fairly long stitch (2.5mm), without pulling on the ribbons at all, so that the seams are really flat. Press if necessary.

PATCHWORK

Bond some iron-on interfacing to the wrong side of the two rectangles of linen.

Fold the remaining 16cm length of patterned ribbon in half. Sew the ends on the right side of the rectangle of linen that will form the back of the bag, centred and 4cm down from the top. Attach the 'made by hand' tape close to the top edge to cover the ribbon ends (see photograph on page 32).

At the base of the other linen rectangle, attach the embroidered tulle and the two 15cm lace trims to make a patchwork 37 x 12cm. Attach the 37cm of ivory lace trim to the top of this patchwork, then, just above, the previously prepared patterned and satin ribbons. Sew the red velvet ribbon, folded in half, to this and attach the flower on top.

ASSEMBLY

Join the two linen rectangles by sewing the sides and the base 1cm from the edges, right sides together. Cut the corners at an angle. Turn right side out and press.

Mark the positions of the handles using pins or tailor's chalk: place them 8cm from the side seams; how high they are positioned will depend upon the type of handles that you have. Sew them using strong sewing thread. To prevent them from getting in the way during the following steps, hold them flat on the linen by using long tacking (basting) stitches or safety pins.

LINING AND FINISHING TOUCHES

Cut the inside pocket from the linen using the pattern provided on page 88 (the seam allowances are included). Attach the fine white lace trim to the right side of the fabric, 6.5cm from the top. Sew the small button to the centre. Oversew the outer edges of the linen. Press a 3.5cm hem along the top edge, then unfold it. Place the elastic into the fold and attach it to the ends with a few stitches in order to gather the pocket. Fold the hem down and sew it 3cm from the edge, keeping the elastic taut.

{TIP}: IF YOU THINK IT WILL BE DIFFICULT TO PLACE THE ELASTIC IN THE INSIDE POCKET AS EXPLAINED ABOVE, STITCH THE HEM FIRST, THREAD THE ELASTIC THROUGH IT WITH THE HELP OF A SAFETY PIN, THEN SEW THE ENDS.

Press a 5mm turning around the raw edges of the pocket. Attach the pocket to the right side of the lining, 7cm from the top edge and centred across the width.

Fold the lining in half, right sides together. Stitch the sides 1cm from the edges, leaving an opening approx. 20cm long along one of the edges.

Insert the bag into the lining, right sides together. Stitch the top 2cm from the edge. Turn right side out. Close the opening in the lining with a line of stitching.

Press the bag, taking care not to touch the handles with the iron. Sew the button onto the front, centred between the handles.

11cm

32cm

35cm

✳ Embroidered shopping bag

Measurements: 42 x 38 x 14cm without the handles

Two times 44 x 26cm of white medium-weight linen for the top of the bag · Unbleached linen: two times 44 x 16cm for the bottom of the bag; two times 16 x 44cm for the side sections · Scraps of linen and cotton in shades of grey and brown for the patchwork · Spotted linen: 44 x 13cm for the back of the bag; two times 16 x 52cm for the pockets · Floral linen for the lining: 44 x 90cm; two times 16 x 39cm · Scraps of lace trim · 44cm of scalloped lace trim, 1.5cm wide · 1.4m of black velvet ribbon, 1cm wide · 2m grey cotton tape, 2.5cm wide · One embroidered heart on tulle, approx. 5cm square · 90 x 60cm of heavyweight iron-on interfacing · One pair of black leather handles with holes for sewing, approx. 70cm long · 22cm of elastic, 2.5cm wide · Strong white sewing thread in silk or linen

For the motif: materials to transfer the motif (see page 88) · Lace fabric roses · One scrap of fine lace · Black stranded embroidery thread

FRONT

Join the pieces of grey and brown fabric to make a strip of patchwork 44 x 13cm.
Attach the embroidered heart tulle to the right end of the patchwork, as well as some vertical lace trims between some of the pieces.
Sew the patchwork in between the white linen and one rectangle of unbleached linen, right sides together, sewing 1cm from the edges.
Attach the scalloped lace, overlapping the patchwork and the white linen, with the scallops facing up.
The motif of the little girl is provided on page 91. Transfer it to the white linen, centred across the width and approx. 2cm up from the patchwork. Embroider it using backstitch. Using the photograph on page 38 for inspiration, attach the lace roses and the scrap of lace forming the girl's skirt.
Press a fold across the unbleached linen 7cm beneath the patchwork (the bottom 8cm will form half the base).
Cut a rectangle of iron-on interfacing 42 x 45cm. Using an iron, bond it to the wrong side of the front of the bag, leaving an allowance of 1cm at the sides and bottom, and 5cm at the top.

BACK

Working as for the front of the bag, join the three back pieces (white linen at the top, spotted linen in the centre, unbleached linen at the bottom). Then stiffen everything with interfacing.

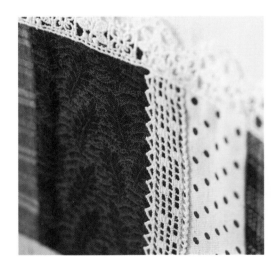

BACKSTITCH

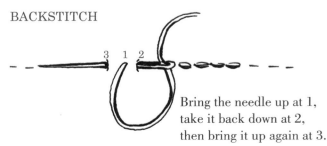

Bring the needle up at 1, take it back down at 2, then bring it up again at 3.

SIDE SECTIONS

Cut two rectangles 14 x 38cm of iron-on interfacing. Attach them to the wrong side of the unbleached linen for the side sections, leaving the same allowances as before.

Fold each of the spotted linen rectangles for the pockets in half lengthways, wrong sides together. Press the folds. Place 11cm of elastic into the fold, attach it to the ends, then encase it by sewing 3cm from the fold. Fold the pocket, right sides together, and sew the bottom 1cm from the edge. Turn right side out and press. Oversew the side edges. Attach 35cm of the black velvet ribbon to each side of the pocket, level with the elastic seam, using a few stitches.

Position the pockets on the right side of the fabric for the side sections, 8cm from the bottom. Sew them close to the edge across the bottom and along the sides.

ASSEMBLY

Join the front of the bag to the back by sewing the base 1cm from the edge, right sides together. Join the side sections 1cm from the edges, wrong sides together (the seams are outside). Position the grey tape, overlapping the side seams: sew it to the outside panels, right sides together, then fold it over the side seams and slipstitch the long edge in place.

Mark the positions of the handles using pins or tailor's chalk. Place them 11cm from the side edges and 11cm up from the patchwork (or the spotted linen at the back). Sew them using strong thread.

To make the lining, sew the large rectangle around the two side sections, right sides together, 1cm from the edges. Press the seams.

Insert the lining into the bag, wrong sides together.

Fold the top edges of the bag down by 2cm, then by 3cm (the top of the lining is not folded; it is flat under the hem). Stitch the hem to the lining by hand using small stitches.

Carefully press the bag, without using steam to prevent the iron-on interfacing from swelling, and taking care not to touch the handles with the iron.

✳ Holdall with scalloped edging

Measurements: 35 x 31cm

Two times 37 x 33cm of unbleached medium-weight linen fabric • 37 x 22cm
of white linen for the flap • 37 x 22cm of white cotton fabric for the flap facing
• Two times 37 x 33cm of patterned cotton fabric for the lining • 18 x 18cm
of linen or white cotton fabric embroidered with a monogram • 50cm of white
lace trim, 1.2cm wide • 70cm of linen string • One metal heart charm, 2cm
high • Pair of compasses

FLAP

Using the pattern provided on page 94, cut one scallop-edged
piece from the white linen and cotton fabrics for the flap and its
facing (seam allowances included).

Centre the compasses on the wrong side of the monogram, trace
a circle 13cm in diameter, then cut it out. Pin it to the right
side of the scalloped flap, centring it carefully.

Attach it by sewing all around, overlapping the edge with a
small zigzag stitch.

Sew a row of stitching along the lace trim using a long running
stitch, then pull the threads to gather it very slightly. Attach it
around the monogram, folding one end over the other to neaten.

Lay the flap and the facing, right sides together. Working 1cm
from the edges, sew the scallops, then sew the sides, stopping
1cm from the top.

Cut the seam allowance around the scallops approx. 5mm from
the row of stitching. Using a pair of sharp pointed scissors, snip
small triangular notches along the curves and nicks into the
points as far as the row of stitching, making sure not to actually
cut the stitching.

Turn the flap right side out, press it, then turn it back right
sides together.

ASSEMBLY

Join the open top edge of the flap to one of the rectangles of
unbleached linen, right sides together, 1cm from the edge.
Repeat, to join the open top edge of the facing to one of the
rectangles of lining.

Lay the second rectangle of unbleached linen and the second
rectangle of lining, right sides together. Sew along the top 1cm
from the edge.

Fold the flap over the linen and pin so that it does not get in
the way during the next stage. Unfold the two linen and lining
pieces and place them right sides together, linen against linen,
and lining against lining. Sew the outer edge 1cm from the
edges, leaving an opening 20cm long at the base of the lining.
Cut the corners at an angle.

Turn right side out. Close up the opening with a neat seam.
Put the lining in place inside the holdall and press.

Pass the linen string through the holes in the lace around the
monogram, then tie it at the bottom, attaching the metal
heart to it.

✳ Little bag

Measurements: diameter approx. 19cm

One crocheted mat in white cotton, approx. 18cm in diameter · 45 x 25cm of unbleached medium-weight linen fabric · 45 x 25cm of patterned cotton fabric for the lining · 1.8m of black lace trim, 1.5cm wide · 50cm of black ribbon, 5mm wide · 1.5m of white linen ribbon with black stitching, 1cm wide · One black button 1.5cm in diameter · One metal heart charm, 1.5cm high · Pair of compasses

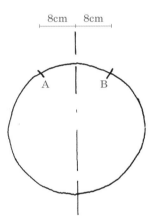

PREPARATION

Trace a circle on some paper with a diameter 1.5cm greater than that of the mat (i.e. 21cm diameter for a mat 18cm in diameter). Cut out the circle, then fold it in half to find the central axis and to mark the straight grain.

Unfold and trace a line along the fold. Mark two points A and B, 8cm either side of the line on the top edge of the circle (see the diagram opposite).

Using this pattern, cut two circles of linen and two circles of lining. Transfer the marks.

DECORATION

Sew the black lace trim around the mat, on the wrong side, so that it overlaps a little; leave about 11cm of the top edge of the mat free of lace.

Attach the mat to the right side of one of the linen circles, using small stitches and centring it.

Thread the black ribbon through one ring of holes in the mat. Thread it up and down through the holes until it comes out again at the front, then tie in a bow and attach the metal heart.

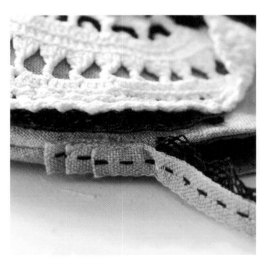

ASSEMBLY

Place each circle of linen on a circle of lining, right sides together. Sew around the edge from point A to point B, 1cm from the edge. Make a nick in the seam allowance at both ends of the stitching.

Lay the two pieces of lining right sides together.

Sew around the edge 1cm from the edge, from one mark to the other, leaving an opening of 15cm at the base.

Lay the two pieces of linen right sides together. Sew them 1cm from the edge, from one mark to the other.

Turn the bag right side out. Sew a line of stitching to close the opening in the lining. Put the lining in place in the little bag, then press.

SHOULDER STRAP

Sew the remaining black lace trim to the linen ribbon, so that it overlaps the width on one side, leaving approx. 9cm of the ribbon free at each end. Fold the ends without lace to make three layers of folds. Position them on the little bag either side of the opening, so that the lace trim is facing forwards. Sew the ends firmly by hand through the folds.

Sew the button onto the top of the linen circle at the front, in the centre of the opening.

✳ Pretty wallet

Measurements: 24 x 17cm

24 x 34cm of white medium-weight linen fabric, for the outside (A) · 24 x 21cm of medium-weight ivory linen fabric for the top part of the inside (B) · 24 x 14cm of floral cotton fabric, for the bottom part of the inside (C) · 22 x 22cm of floral cotton for the appliqué pocket (D) · 24 x 33cm of ivory patchwork fabric for the integrated pocket (E) · Seven lace trims in different widths and 34cm long, to produce a colour gradation from white to beige 16cm wide · 50cm of lace trim, 1.2cm wide · 24cm of ribbon woven with initials, 1cm wide · 1 tape woven with the inscription 'made by hand' · 2m of ivory tape, 2cm wide · One lace flower, approx. 6cm high · One embroidered monogram, approx. 7cm high · 60 x 60cm of lightweight iron-on interfacing · One ivory zipper, 22cm long · One silver button, 1.8cm in diameter · One flat pearlized button, 1.5cm in diameter · One small sew-on press stud

PREPARATION

Using an iron, attach the iron-on interfacing to the wrong side of pieces A, B, C and D.
On the right side of the linen fabric A, centre and sew the seven lace trims to make a colour-gradated band 16cm wide.

APPLIQUÉ POCKET

Cut 50cm of the ivory tape. Make layered folds of approx. 8mm until the tape is 22cm long. Sew the folds in place close to one long edge (see the photo on page 49).
Fold the floral fabric D in half, right sides together.
Place the folded tape between the two layers of fabric along the long open side, with the folds facing inside. Sew 1cm from the edge.
Turn the pocket right side out and press. Oversew the edges of both open sides through both layers.
At the bottom of the pocket, position the initialled ribbon where it looks nicest, depending on the pattern of your fabric, and attach by hand.
Pin the pocket to the right side of linen B, 3cm from the short side at the top. Tack (baste) the 1.2cm wide lace trim around the side and bottom edges. Sew through all the thicknesses.
Sew the flat pearlized button onto the top front of the pocket and attach the press stud beneath, on the inside of the pocket.

INTEGRATED POCKET

Taking your inspiration from the photograph on page 47, arrange the monogram, lace flower and 'made by hand' tape nicely on the floral fabric C. Attach them by hand.

Fold a 1cm turning to the wrong side of the two short sides of fabric E. With the right sides together, fold up the bottom by 11.5cm and the top by 4cm. Press the folds with an iron. Sew the zipper to the two short edges of fabric E: it is placed with the right side of the zipper to the wrong side of the fabric (diagram 1).

Attach the fabrics B and C to each side of the zipper piece (diagram 2). To make this look nice and easier to do, it is better to work by hand, with small, even running stitches.

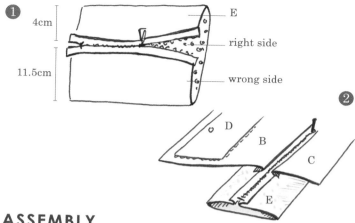

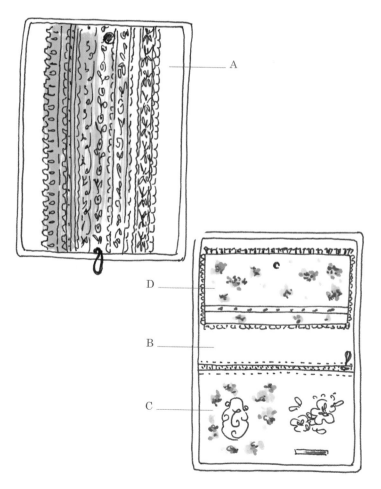

ASSEMBLY

Place the inside pieces on linen A, wrong sides together. Tack (baste) the outer edge through all the thicknesses, carefully lining up the edges (trim them slightly if necessary to make an even rectangle).

To make the button loop, cut a piece of ivory tape 12cm long. Fold the ends inside, fold the tape in half lengthways, and sew to close the long edge close to the edge. Fold the loop in half and attach it to linen A, in the centre of the bottom edge. Sew on the button, facing it, on the opposite side.

To achieve a neat finish, cut the four corners of the piece, rounding them slightly. Stitch the ivory tape all around the edges on the inside, right sides together.

Fold the tape to the outside and sew it by hand using slip stitch. Press the wallet through a light terry towel to avoid crushing the embroidery and the lace.

3. Celebrations

Decorative wreath

Pretty wicker basket

Decorative candleholder

Place setting

Soft pompoms

Attractive cones

✳ Decorative wreath

One wreath in bleached willow, 25cm in diameter • Approx. 2m of unbleached linen fabric, 3cm wide (cut a strip along the selvedge or join several strips together end to end) • Cotton twill tape, 2cm wide: 2m in white; 60cm in beige • Two of ivory lace trim, 1.5cm wide • 60cm of white lace trim, 1.5cm wide • Scraps of organza ribbon • Eight white buttons in different sizes

For the flowers: 40 x 15cm of unbleached linen fabric • 40 x 15cm of white cotton fabric • 40 x 15cm of stiff transparent fabric such as organdie • 4m of ivory tape, 2cm wide • 90 x 25cm of heavyweight iron-on interfacing • Strong white sewing thread in silk or linen

Wind the white cotton twill tape around the wreath, ending with a bow at the base.
Lightly fray the linen strip by scratching the edges with your fingernails. Wind it around the wreath crossing over the serge trim. Wind the ivory lace trim following the linen strip. Tie the ends of the linen and lace in a bow at the base of the wreath.

FLOWERS
Make four pleated flowers using the ivory tape, proceeding as explained on page 28. Reinforce the linen and the white cotton for the flowers by bonding the iron-on interfacing to the reverse using an iron. Using the patterns provided on page 90, cut two large petals and two small ones from each of the stiffened fabrics; also cut four small petals from the transparent fabric. Place two small petals onto each of the large ones, varying the order in which you lay them. Sew them together with a few small stitches in the centre, and then sew the pleated flowers on top.

Fix the flowers firmly to the wreath with the strong thread. Sew on the buttons, spacing them apart nicely, and tie the organza ribbons around them.

HANGING LOOP
Fold the beige cotton twill tape in half along the length and press. Insert the white lace trim into the fold, then stitch the edges together to secure it. Firmly attach the hanging loop to the top of the wreath.

✳ Pretty wicker basket

One oval basket measuring approx. 1.1m around the perimeter and 50cm in height (including the handle) · Embroidered edging in white cotton, 5cm wide: length equal to the perimeter of the basket · Three or four strips of linen and lace long enough to wrap around the handle, 2cm wide · One scrap of embroidered tulle and one scrap of lace for the top of the handle · Strong white sewing thread in silk or linen

For the flower: 40 x 20cm of white linen or cotton fabric · 50 x 16cm of white tulle · 30cm of two different lace trims, 2cm wide · One small lace flower motif · Some white pearlized beads

For the cover: White cotton fabric: (perimeter of the basket + 10cm) x 25cm · Embroidered scalloped edging in white cotton, 6cm wide: same length as the cotton fabric · Narrow white ribbon: length of the cotton fabric + 30cm

Using the strong thread, sew the embroidered edging around the main basket by passing the needle between the twigs. Wrap the strips of linen and lace around the handle. Attach them firmly with a few stitches at the base. Tie the scraps of embroidered tulle and lace to the top of the handle.

FLOWER

Using the patterns provided on pages 90–91, cut three petals in different sizes from the white fabric. Lay them on top of one another in decreasing order, then add the flower in lace on top. Hold everything together with a few stitches in the centre and sew on the beads. Fold the two lace trims in half, fix them to the back of the flower and cut them so that the ends are different lengths. Fold the tulle in half along the length to make a strip 50 x 8cm. Sew the long open sides together using long stitches, then gather up by pulling the threads. Join the short sides and sew the tulle underneath the flower. Attach the whole thing to the front of the basket, just above the embroidered edging.

COVER

At the top of the cotton fabric, fold a double to the right side to make a casing: 1cm, then 1.5cm. Push the fabric inside the hem at both ends. Press the hem, fold the scalloped edging underneath, then sew close to the bottom fold.
Fold the cotton in half, right sides together. Sew the sides together 1cm from the edge, stopping level with the hem. Make a small hem around the bottom edge.

Turn the cover right side out and press. Thread the ribbon into the casing with the help of a safety pin.
Place the cover inside the basket, lining up the bottom edge with the embroidered edging on the outside. Using the strong thread, sew it firmly at this level and then again, level with the upper edge of the basket.

✳ Decorative candleholder

One candleholder 8–9cm in diameter · 30 x 30cm of unbleached medium-weight linen fabric · 30 x 30cm of floral linen fabric · 35 x 20cm of white cotton fabric · 10 x 10cm of iron-on interfacing · Four buttons 1.5cm in diameter · 1m of linen string

For the flower: 10 x 15cm of white fabric · 10 x 15cm of floral fabric · Scrap of embroidered tulle · 10 x 15cm of iron-on interfacing

DECORATIVE SURROUND

Cut the unbleached linen and the floral linen using the pattern provided on page 90 (seam allowances of 5mm included).
Lay them, right sides together. Sew the outer edge 5mm from the edge, leaving an opening of around 6cm.
Turn right side out. Turn the edges of the opening inside and close them with small stitches. Press.
To make the drawstring channel, make two rows of stitching spaced 1cm apart following the dotted lines on the pattern.
On the unbleached linen, make two small vertical incisions across the drawstring channel, on opposite sides of the shape (they will enable the tie-strings to be passed through).
Cut two circles 16cm in diameter from the white cotton fabric.
Cut a circle 8cm in diameter from the iron-on interfacing as well as from a piece of paper. Using an iron, bond the circle of iron-on interfacing to the wrong side of one of the circles of cotton, centring it correctly.
Lay the two circles of cotton, right sides together. Sew the outer edge close to the edge, leaving an opening of around 6cm long.
Turn right side out. Push the edges of the opening to the inside and close them with small stitches. Press.
Place the circles of cotton in the centre of the decorative surround on the unbleached linen side. Pin the paper circle in the centre. Sew all around through all the thicknesses.
Topstitch four lines, 2cm long, in the shape of a star, around the stitched circle, as indicated on the pattern.
Sew a button at the end of each line of topstitching.
Remove the paper circle.

Cut the string into two equal lengths. Thread them through the drawstring channel with the help of a safety pin: pass the first string right round the channel through one opening and tie a knot in the end, then repeat, using the opposite opening with the other string.

FLOWER

Reinforce the white fabric by bonding the iron-on interfacing to the reverse. Using the pattern provided on page 90, cut a small petal from the white fabric and another from the floral fabric. Place the floral petal onto the white petal, add a smaller one cut from the tulle, then hold everything together with a few stitches in the centre. Now sew this flower firmly to the knot on one of the drawstrings.

FINISHING TOUCHES

Place the candleholder into the decorative surround, then draw it up by pulling on the strings.

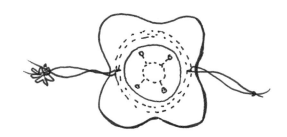

✳ Place setting

Measurements: 16 x 28cm

25 x 30cm of unbleached linen fabric · 25 x 35cm of white linen fabric ·
40 x 35cm of white cotton fabric for the lining · 30cm of white lace trim,
1.2cm wide · 10cm of white lace trim, 8cm wide · 8cm of embroidered edging
in white cotton, 6cm wide · One embroidered monogram, approx. 6cm high ·
40 x 35cm of lightweight, iron-on interfacing · 60cm of linen string

Using an iron, bond the iron-on interfacing to the wrong side
of the cotton fabric for the lining. Join the two parts of the
pattern provided on pages 88–89 (seam allowances included).
Cut pattern A once from the unbleached linen and pattern B
once from the white linen. Cut each of the two patterns once
from the stiffened lining (diagram 1).

Attach the 8cm lace trim to the base of the unbleached linen,
then attach the 6cm embroidered edging to its base. Attach
the monogram 1.5cm above the lace.

Lay the white linen and the corresponding lining, right sides
together. Sew the scallops between points E and F, 5mm from
the edge. In the seam allowance, make a small nick at points
C, D, E and F (diagram 2).

Lay the unbleached linen and the corresponding lining, right
sides together. Sew across the top 1cm from the edge. Press the
seam allowances flat.

Unfold both joined pieces and lay them on top of one another,
right sides together, the linen against the linen and the lining
against the lining. Sew the outer edge 1cm from the edges,
leaving an opening of 10cm long on the lining (diagram 3). Cut
the corners at an angle. Turn the piece right side out and press.
Push the edges of the opening inside and close them with small
stitches. Put the lining in place in the pouch.

Attach the 1.2cm lace trim around the pouch. Thread the string
through the holes in the lace, then tie the ends together,
slightly drawing in the pouch.

{TIP}: YOU CAN USE THESE PLACE SETTINGS TO
GIVE A LITTLE GIFT TO EACH OF YOUR GUESTS.

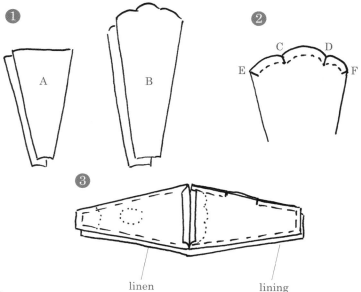

❶

❷

A

B

C   D

E   F

❸

linen   lining

✳ Soft pompoms

Scraps of unbleached linen fabric, white cotton fabric and embroidered tulle
• Lace trims in different widths, at least 1m long • Fine string • 30 x 15cm
of thick card (for example, from a shoe box)

PREPARATION
Cut the pattern provided on page 93 twice from the cardboard.
Cut strips measuring 1 or 2cm wide by at least 1m long from
the linen, cotton and tulle.

POMPOM
Lay the two circles of cardboard on top of each other. Cut a
1m length of string and insert it between the circles of card,
avoiding the central hole and so that the ends emerge at the
same point on the edge of the card. Wrap the strips of fabric
and the lace trims around the card through the central hole,
alternating the fabrics and keeping the string in place. Do
this in such a way that each strip and each trim starts and
finishes on the outside edge of the circles (or trim them if
necessary). Continue in this way until the centre hole of the
circles is filled.

Hold onto the string and start to cut the fabrics and the trims,
progressing from the string ends around the perimeter. Then
immediately draw the string up between the two pieces of card
and tie firmly in a double knot. Remove the card.

Fluff up the pompon and make it even by trimming fringes
if necessary.

✳ Attractive cones

Measurements: diameter 7cm x height 22cm

One papier mâché cone, 7cm in diameter and 18cm high (sold in handicraft shops) · 30 x 25cm of linen or cotton fabric, white or beige · Scraps of lace trims and ribbons · 40cm of lace trim or ribbon for hanging · Embroidered monograms, lace motifs, découpage images, buttons, etc. · 30 x 25cm of iron-on interfacing · Pearlized round beads · Strong white sewing thread in silk or linen · Stiff nylon thread · Strong PVA adhesive, in a tube with a fine nozzle · Large needle, pegs, hole punch, cocktail sticks, pinking shears

For the trim: 30 x 25cm of transparent fabric (linen gauze, tulle) · 30cm of lace edging · 30cm of fine ribbon · Dried flowers or bath salts

For the flower with pistils: 10 x 10cm of slightly frayed fine fabric (organdie, raw silk) · A few flower pistils (sold in handicraft shops or haberdashers' shops) · Spray starch

PREPARATION

Thread 30cm of strong thread onto the large needle. Sew right through the base of the papier mâché cone, approx. 1.5cm from the tip. Leave the needle hanging.

Make a small bouquet of lace trims and ribbons, decorated with beads threaded onto some nylon thread.

Attach the bouquet firmly to the base of the cone using the large needle. Add a drop of adhesive, then hold it in place with a peg whilst it dries. Punch two holes opposite each other 1cm from the top of the cone. Thread the lace trim or hanging ribbon through them. Glue or staple the ends into the cone, then hide them beneath a strip of paper or a ribbon.

Attach some iron-on interfacing to the wrong side of the linen or cotton fabric. Then cut out one piece for the cone from the pattern provided on page 93. Cut a zigzag edging along the top edge. Sew or glue the decorations of your choice in the centre.

LOOPS OF BEADS

Cut a piece of nylon thread approx. 15cm long, thread on a bead, place a drop of adhesive inside the bead using a cocktail stick and leave to dry. Thread the remaining beads in the same way, spacing them apart. Once the adhesive is dry, fold the thread into a loop, slip the ends under the decorations and fix them firmly in place with some stitches and adhesive.

{TIP}: YOU CAN MAKE THE BASIC CONE YOURSELF USING
FLEXIBLE CARDBOARD OR STIFFENED FABRIC, AND
REFERRING TO THE PATTERN.

FLOWER WITH PISTILS

Spray the fabric with starch. Cut out a small flower using the pattern provided on page 89. Pierce the hole in the centre. Place a thin line of adhesive on the grey areas of the pattern, working from the centre to the outside. Glue the side of each petal to its neighbour (diagram 1). Leave to dry. Sew the pistils into the central hole, glue, then tie everything together at the base (diagram 2).

ASSEMBLY

Fold the tip of the decorated linen or cotton fabric to the wrong side, by 1.5cm, and glue. Using the pinking shears, cut the side that will overlap the other one. Place thin lines of adhesive on the outer edge of the papier mâché cone and carefully wrap the decorated linen or cotton around it.
Hold the tip and the edge in place using pegs, until they dry.

LINING

Cut one piece of transparent fabric using the pattern for the cone. Then remove 1cm all around the edge. Attach the lace edging around the top. Fold this lining in half, right sides together, and stitch the open side. Turn right side out. Fill the lining with dried flowers or bath salts, close it by tying the fine ribbon around it, then slip it inside the cone.

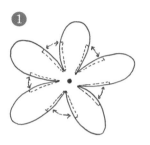

4. Little gifts

Bag on a chain

Stole

Lavender pillows

Purse

Delicate gift bags

Beautiful boxes

✳ Bag on a chain

Measurements: 20 x 16cm without the handle

30 x 40cm of unbleached linen fabric · 30 x 40cm of floral cotton fabric · 60cm of ivory lace trim, 1.5cm wide · 30 x 40cm of lightweight wadding (batting) · One chain for a small bag, 25cm long, with clip fasteners · Flat-nosed pliers for tightening the clips

For the flower: 15 x 15cm of thick white cotton fabric · 15 x 15cm of unbleached linen fabric · 15 x 15cm of transparent fabric (gauze or organdie) · 20 x 15cm of iron-on interfacing · Three buttons.

PREPARATION

Using the pattern provided on page 92, cut two pieces of linen, two pieces of floral cotton and two pieces of wadding (batting) (seam allowances are included).

ASSEMBLY

For each of the two sides of the bag, place a piece of linen and a piece of cotton, right sides together, and place a piece of wadding (batting) on top. Sew the outer edge 1cm from the edges, leaving an opening, 8cm long, at the base. Cut the corners at an angle. Turn the two bags right side out and press. Sew the lace trim to the wrong side of one of the bags, around the two sides and the base.

Lay the two bags, floral cotton against floral cotton, and pin them together. Join the two sides and the base by hand, close to the edge, using a tight running stitch.

FLOWER

Reinforce the cotton and linen for the flower by bonding iron-on interfacing to the reverse using an iron. Using the patterns provided on page 90, cut a large petal from the white cotton, a small petal from the unbleached linen and a small petal from the transparent fabric. Place the two small petals onto the large one, ending with the transparent one. Sew the three buttons to the centre to hold everything together.

FINISHING TOUCHES

Sew the flower to the centre of the front of the bag.
Attach the chain to each side of the opening with the help of the flat-nosed pliers.

✳ Stole

Measurements: 20cm x 1.34m

22cm x 1.16m of lightweight ivory linen fabric · 22cm x 1.16m of lightweight white cotton fabric · Two times 22 x 12cm of lightweight beige linen fabric · Two times 22 x 12cm of lightweight floral cotton fabric · 44cm of lace trim, 2cm wide · Two small embroidered discs cut from an embroidered edging.

For the brooch: One steel kilt pin with loops, 5cm long · Thick embroidery thread (e.g. cotton perlé) · Three metal charms · Lace motifs

STOLE

Join the two pieces of floral cotton fabric to the ends of the ivory linen, right sides together, sewing 1cm from the edges. Cut the lace trim into two equal lengths. Attach them to the ivory linen, just above the joining seams.
Working as before, join the two pieces of beige linen to the ends of the white cotton fabric.
Lay the two joined pieces, right sides together.
Sew around the outer edge 1cm from the edge, leaving an opening 12cm long on one of the sides.
Cut the corners at an angle.
Turn the stole right side out and press. Turn the edges of the opening inside, then close them up using small stitches.
Attach the two small embroided discs by hand, centred on the lace trims.

BROOCH

Wrap some embroidery thread around the pin. Thread the charms and the scraps of lace through the loops on the kilt pin. Attach the lace motifs to the embroidery thread firmly using several stitches.

D = BACK FLAPS

✳ Lavender pillows

Measurements: 16 x 16.5cm without the handles

Fabrics: 11 x 16cm for the front (A); Two times 4.5 x 16cm for the side strips (B); Two times 16 x 4.5cm for the top and bottom strips (C); Two times 16 x 15cm for the back flaps (D) • 16 x 34cm of white cotton fabric for the cushion pad • 11cm of three different white lace trims, 2 or 3cm wide • 44cm of string • Embroidery thread in silk or cotton, red • Wadding (batting) • Loose dried lavender • Materials for transferring the embroidery motifs (see page 88)

Pieces: A and D in unbleached linen (alt. white linen); B in white linen (alt. floral cotton linen); C in ivory cotton (alt. unbleached linen).

COVER

Choose the letters and motifs from page 92. Transfer them to linen A, at the centre top. Embroider them in long stitch and running stitch.

Attach the three lace trims, overlapping them approx. 1.5cm below the embroidery.

Join the two strips B either side of the embroidered linen, right sides together, 1cm from the edges. Press.

Fold each strip C in half along the length, wrong sides together. Press the fold using an iron, then unfold.

Join one strip to the base of the central piece, right sides together, 1cm from the edge. Press. Join the other strip to the top in the same way, inserting the ends of a piece of string 22cm long to make a handle (diagram 1). Press and oversew the outer edges.

By sewing as before, join one flap D to the bottom of strip C and the other flap D to the top of strip C, inserting a piece of string 22cm long (diagram 2). Oversew the edges of the ends of the flaps, then fold them over by 4cm, to make hems on the wrong side.

Unfold the piece, with the right side uppermost. Re-fold the top edge, then the bottom edge, along the folds pressed into both C strips, right sides together. Pin the sides and sew them 1cm from the edges through all the layers. Cut the corners at an angle. Turn right side out. Carefully push out the corners using the point of a pair of scissors.

Press, taking care not to crush the embroidery.

LONG STITCH

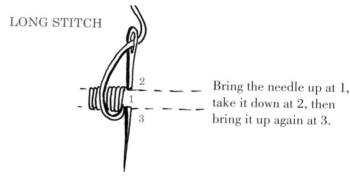

Bring the needle up at 1, take it down at 2, then bring it up again at 3.

CUSHION PAD

Fold the cotton fabric in half along the length, right sides together. Sew the three open sides, leaving an opening 10cm long on one of them. Turn the cushion right side out and press. Then fill it with wadding (batting) mixed with lavender. Turn the edges of the opening inside and close them up with small stitches.

Insert the cushion pad into the cover.

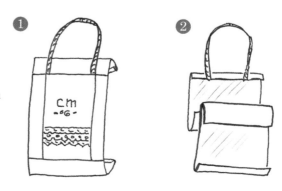

✳ Purse

45 x 20cm of white linen fabric · 45 x 20cm of floral cotton fabric for the lining · 18cm of beige lace trim, 1cm wide · Three scraps of white and ivory lace trims, 1cm wide · One metal purse clasp, for sewing, 8cm wide · Rocaille beads · One copper button, 1.5cm in diameter · Strong adhesive for fabric and metal · Pegs

PREPARATION

The patterns are provided on page 95 (seam allowances are included; they are 5mm for the whole piece). Cut pattern A twice and pattern B once from the linen and from the lining. Make notches at points C and D.

For the linen and for the lining, join pieces A either side of piece B, right sides together, leaving 5mm free at the start and at the end, by sewing between points E and F (diagram 1). Make a small notch at the ends of the stitching. Press the seams.

DECORATION

Attach the beige lace trim to piece A in linen, which will be the front of the purse, just beneath notches C and D. Fold a scrap of white lace in half and attach it to the right side using a few stitches, beneath the beige lace.

PURSE AND LINING

Fold the linen piece, right sides together. Sew the sides from C to C' and from D to D'. Press the seams. Close up the corners of the base, carefully making sure that the seams line up at a right angle (diagram 2). Proceed in the same way with the lining, but leaving an opening of 5cm on one of the sides.

Place the linen and the lining right sides together. On each side, sew the top between points C and D. Make notches in the seam allowances along the curves. Turn the piece right side out. Close the opening of the lining using small stitches. Put the lining in place inside the purse. Press the seams at the top.

CLASP

Open the clasp and place a thin line of adhesive in the corner of the frame. Glue it to one of the edges of the purse and hold everything in place using pegs whilst it is drying. Proceed in the same way when attaching the other edge.

Sew the purse to the clasp: starting from the inside, sew through all the thicknesses of fabric, bringing the needle out of a hole in the frame, thread on a rocaille bead and pass the needle back inside through the same hole; continue in the same way from hole to hole.

FINISHING TOUCHES

Fold the two remaining scraps of lace in half. Sew them to the centre of the beige lace, then attach the button on top.

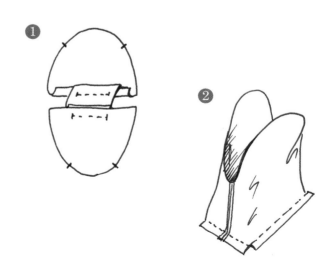

✳ Delicate gift bags

Model 1 (photograph on opposite page). Measurements: 8 x 19 x 3cm
18 x 23cm of white or unbleached linen fabric · 18cm of white or ivory lace trim,
for the top · 20cm of ribbon in white or ivory lace, for the tie · One motif or one
embroidered monogram, approx. 5cm high · One metal charm, approx. 2cm high
· Scrap of card · PVA adhesive

Model 2 (photographs on pages 80 and 82). Measurements: 15 x 16cm
17 x 44cm of white cotton organdie · 17cm of wide lace trim or embroidered
or lace motifs · 40cm of white cotton twill tape, 2cm wide · 2 small
white pompoms

Model 3 (photograph on page 83). Measurements: 11 x 29.5cm
 13 x 31cm of unbleached linen fabric · 13cm of fine ivory lace trim · One
metal heart-shaped button with two holes, 2.5cm wide · 60cm of string

MODEL 1

Oversew the top edge of the linen (i.e. one of the short sides),
then sew on the lace. Fold the linen in half, wrong sides
together, to make a rectangle 9 x 23cm.

Attach the motif or the monogram to the centre of the front
piece, 8cm from the bottom.

Fold the linen, right sides together. Sew the open side and the
base 1cm from the edges, then oversew the edges. Press. Stand
the little bag upright, pinch in the sides at the base and sew
1.5cm from the points (diagram opposite).

Turn the little bag right side out. Measure the base, cut a
rectangle of card to these measurements and glue it into
the little bag.

Thread the charm onto the lace ribbon and tie the ribbon
around the little bag.

{TIP}: IF YOU ARE GIVING A GIFT OF TEA, COFFEE,
BATH SALTS, ETC., MAKE A LITTLE BAG FROM
CHEESECLOTH OR ORGANDIE, A LITTLE SMALLER,
SO IT WILL SLIP INSIDE THE DECORATED
GIFT BAG.

MODEL 2

Oversew the edges of the fabric. Fold it in half, wrong sides together, to form a rectangle 17 x 22cm. Attach the lace trim or the embroidered motifs to the front piece, leaving at least 12cm free at the top.

Fold the fabric, right sides together. Sew the sides 1cm from the edges, leaving a 2cm opening, 12cm from the bottom, on one of them. Turn the little bag right side out. Press.

Fold the top inside by 6cm. Sew two horizontal, parallel rows of stitching either side of the opening on the side to make the drawstring channel.

Fold the cotton tape in half along the length and sew the long edges together.

Thread the tape into the channel with the help of a safety pin. Attach the pompons to the ends with a few tight stitches.

MODEL 3

Oversew the edges of the linen. Fold it in half, wrong sides together, to form a rectangle 13 x 15.5cm. Press the fold. Make a single hem of 1.5cm on the two top edges, on the wrong side, to make a casing. Thread the lace through the holes of the button, then attach it to the front of the little bag. Fold the linen, right sides together. Sew the sides 1cm from the edges, stopping just before the casings. Press.

Cut the corners at an angle. Turn the little bag right side out and press.

Cut the string into two equal lengths. Using a safety pin, thread one half right around the casing and cut the same side; thread the other half in the same way through the opposite opening. Tie the ends of the strings together at each side.

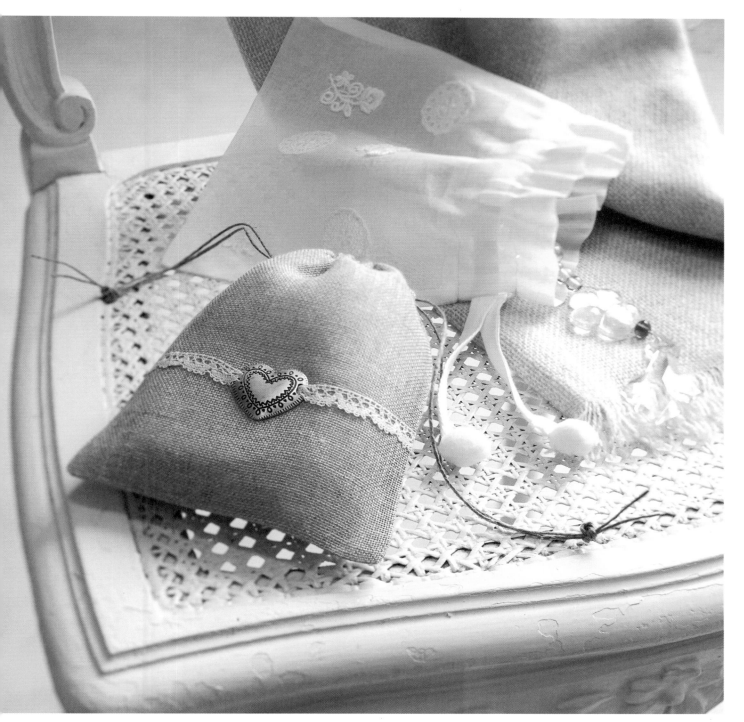

✳ Beautiful boxes

For both models: One cardboard box with lid, 14 x 14cm • 30 x 30cm of floral fabric for the cushion pad • 60cm of lace trim, 1.5cm wide, for the edges of the box • 10cm of two different lace trims, 1cm wide • 25 x 25cm of double-sided iron-on interfacing • 20 x 20cm of lightweight felt • 16 x 16cm of thick felt • 14 x 14cm of mountboard • PVA adhesive, in a tube with a fine nozzle

For the pink model: 25 x 25cm of pink linen fabric • 10 x 10cm of fine unbleached linen • Two times 10 x 10cm of slightly frayed fine fabric (organdie, raw silk): white and pink • 65cm of floral trim, 1cm wide, for the sides of the lid • Two flower motifs in lace: one approx. 7cm high, the other approx. 2cm in diameter • One ornamental button 1.2cm in diameter • A few flower pistils (sold in handicraft and haberdashers' shops) • Stranded embroidery tweed • Spray starch • Materials for transferring the embroidered motif (see page 88)

For the floral model: 25 x 25cm of floral cotton fabric • 25cm of lace trim, 2.5cm wide • One embroidered monogram, approx. 6cm high • One ornamental button 1.5cm in diameter

PINK LID

Choose a letter from the alphabet provided on page 92. Transfer it to the centre of the natural linen. Using two strands of thread, embroider it in long stitch (see page 73) and running stitch. Cut the linen to form a square with 7cm sides. Using the fine fabrics, make two flowers with pistils as explained on page 65.

Pin the embroidered linen to the centre of the pink linen. Place the large lace flower and the two flowers with pistils in the lower left corner of the embroidery. Arrange it so that it looks nice as you position it all on the lid.

Attach the embroidered linen, working by hand using running stitch, then attach the small lace flower in the upper right corner. Attach the large lace flower. Sew the flowers with pistils, then add the button and the two scraps of lace trim folded in half.

FLORAL LID

Attach the lace trim and the monogram to the centre of the floral cotton for the lid, working by hand. Sew the button, placing the two scraps of lace trim folded in half underneath it.

ASSEMBLY AND FINISHING TOUCHES

Attach the double-sided iron-on interfacing, centrally, to the reverse of the decorated cotton or linen. Remove the protective film. Cut the corners at an angle so that you can fold back the sides without too much thickness.

Cut the fine felt to the exact measurements of the lid, then place it on the double-sided iron-on interfacing. Put the lid on the felt top side down. Fold the edges of the linen or cotton over the sides and to the inside of the lid, smoothing them down well. Glue a square of mountboard in the base of the lid to make a neat finish.

For the pink model, glue the floral ribbon around the edges of the lid.

Glue the lace trim around the sides of the main box. Make a small pad according to the inside measurements of the box, wrapping the thick felting in the floral fabric without sewing. Glue it to the bottom of the box.

✳ Patterns

USING THE PATTERNS

All the patterns are provided full size, with seam allowances included. Sometimes a pattern may only represent half of the shape. In such cases, place it on fabric folded in half, lining up the dotted lines on the fold of the fabric.

When a pattern is given in two parts, join them along the dotted lines with some adhesive tape to make the complete shape.

TRANSFERRING A MOTIF FOR EMBROIDERY

You can choose from three methods.

1. Use a motif transfer kit. Following the manufacturer's instructions, trace the motif onto the gauze provided, place it on the fabric and iron the lines traced using a soluble ink pen.
2. Place a photocopy of the motif against a window pane, lay the fabric on top and draw the design that shows through.
3. Photocopy the motif, cut it out and place it under the fabric. Trace the contours, remove the paper, then draw the details freehand.

For the last two methods, work using a pencil with a fine lead or a soluble ink pen, designed for use with textiles.

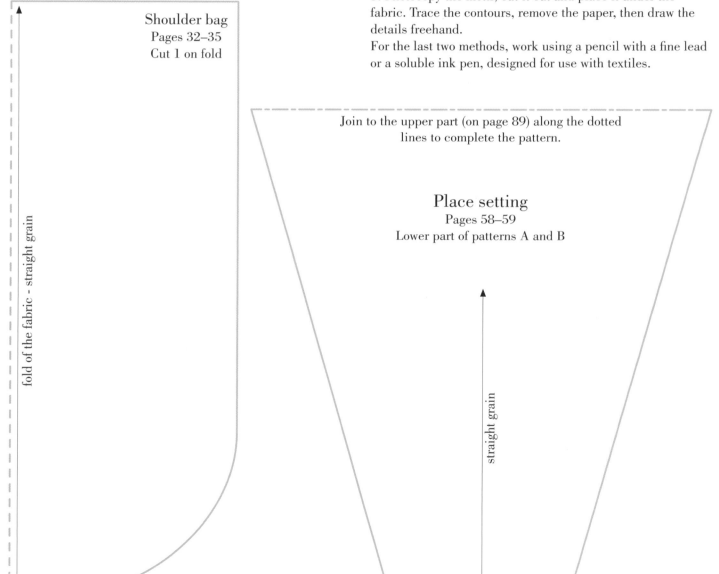

Shoulder bag
Pages 32–35
Cut 1 on fold

fold of the fabric - straight grain

Join to the upper part (on page 89) along the dotted lines to complete the pattern.

Place setting
Pages 58–59
Lower part of patterns A and B

straight grain

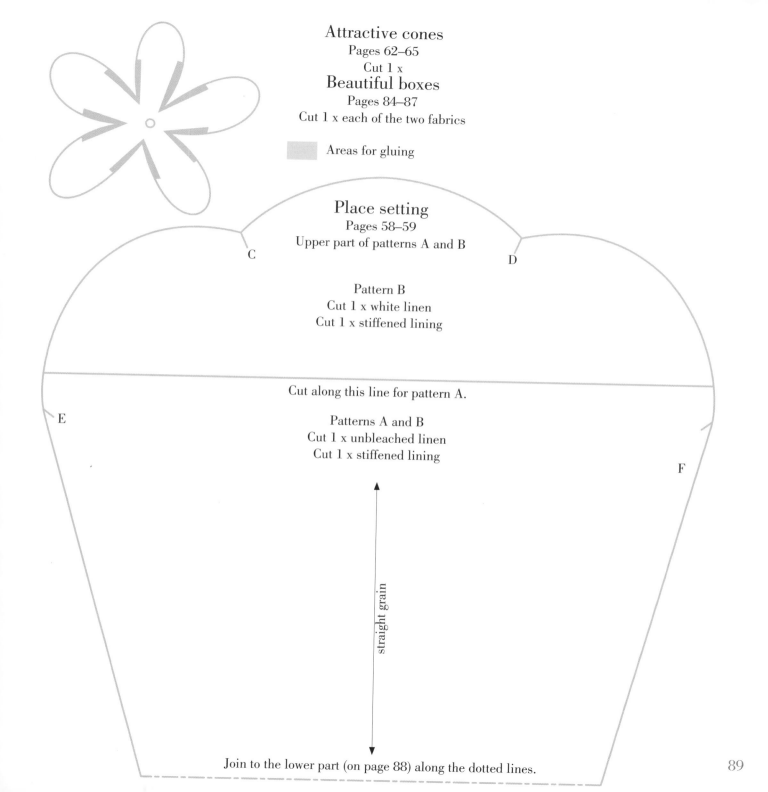

Attractive cones
Pages 62–65
Cut 1 x
Beautiful boxes
Pages 84–87
Cut 1 x each of the two fabrics

Areas for gluing

Place setting
Pages 58–59
Upper part of patterns A and B

C

D

Pattern B
Cut 1 x white linen
Cut 1 x stiffened lining

Cut along this line for pattern A.

Patterns A and B
Cut 1 x unbleached linen
Cut 1 x stiffened lining

E

F

straight grain

Join to the lower part (on page 88) along the dotted lines.

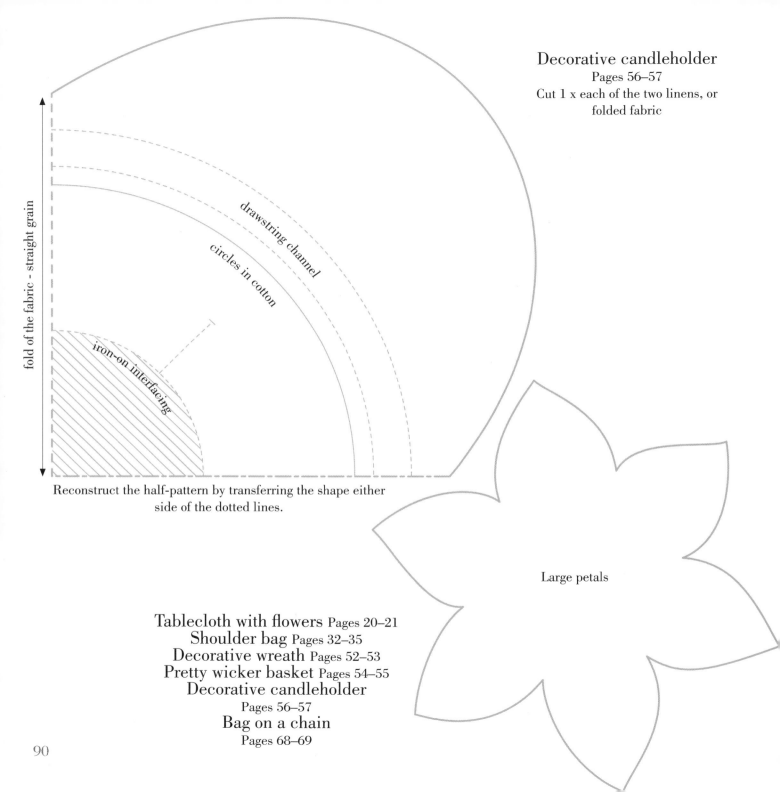

Decorative candleholder
Pages 56–57
Cut 1 x each of the two linens, or folded fabric

fold of the fabric - straight grain

drawstring channel

circles in cotton

iron-on interfacing

Reconstruct the half-pattern by transferring the shape either side of the dotted lines.

Large petals

Tablecloth with flowers Pages 20–21
Shoulder bag Pages 32–35
Decorative wreath Pages 52–53
Pretty wicker basket Pages 54–55
Decorative candleholder
Pages 56–57
Bag on a chain
Pages 68–69

Embroidered
shopping bag
Pages 36–39

Pretty wicker basket
Pages 54–55
Cut 1

Small petals

fold of the fabric - straight grain

Lavender pillows
Pages 72–75
Beautiful boxes
Pages 84–87

Bag on a chain
Pages 68–69
Cut 2 x linen
Cut 2 x lining
Cut 2 x felting

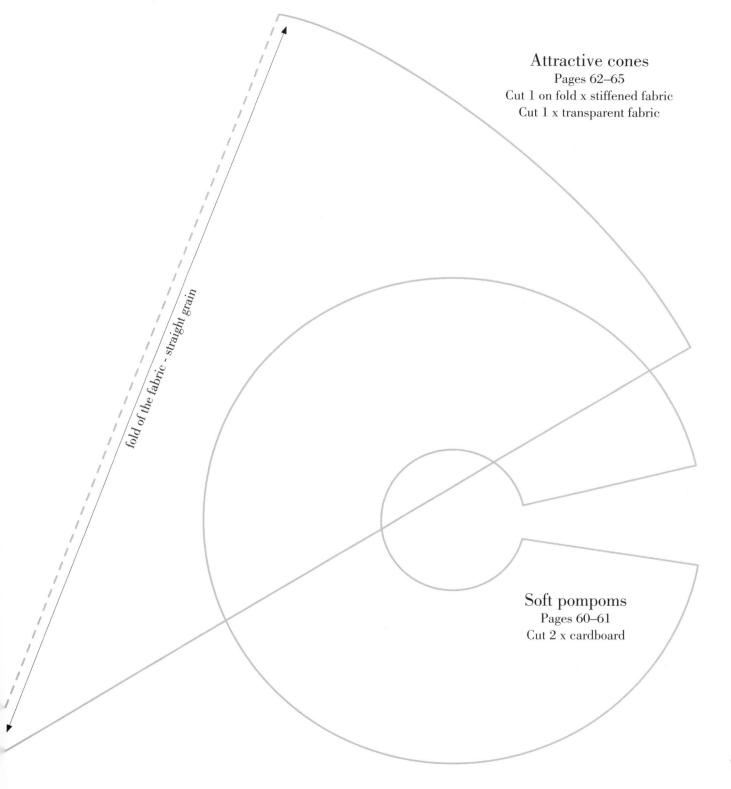

fold of the fabric - straight grain

Attractive cones
Pages 62–65
Cut 1 on fold x stiffened fabric
Cut 1 x transparent fabric

Soft pompoms
Pages 60–61
Cut 2 x cardboard

93

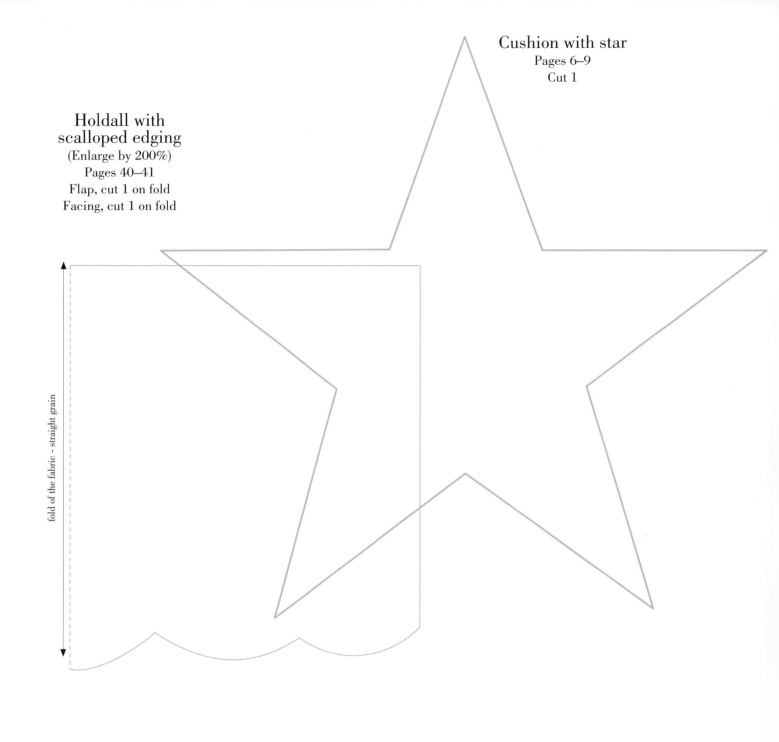

Cushion with star
Pages 6–9
Cut 1

**Holdall with
scalloped edging**
(Enlarge by 200%)
Pages 40–41
Flap, cut 1 on fold
Facing, cut 1 on fold

fold of the fabric - straight grain

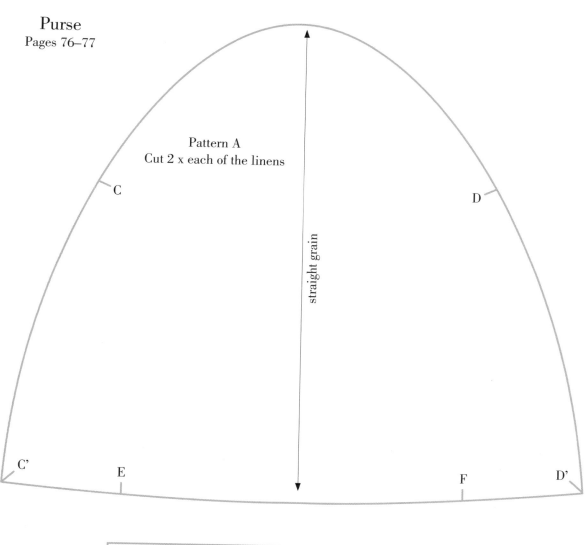

Purse
Pages 76–77

Pattern A
Cut 2 x each of the linens

C

D

straight grain

C'   E   F   D'

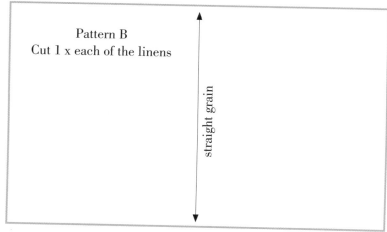

Pattern B
Cut 1 x each of the linens

straight grain

✳ Suppliers

UK

Calico Laine
0151 336 3939
www.calicolaine.co.uk
For fabrics, trimmings and
haberdashery

Cloth House
020 72871555
www.clothhouse.com
For beautiful trims and a wide range
of fabrics

Cowslip Workshops
01566 772654
www.cowslipworkshops.com
For fabrics, especially linen

Gutermann
020 85891642
www.gutermann.com
For high-quality sewing threads

Josy Rose
0845 450 1212
www.josyrose.com
For a wide selection of trimmings

MacCulloch & Wallis
020 7629 0311
www.macculloch-wallis.co.uk
For haberdashery and trimmings,
including bridal fabrics

Millcroft Textiles
0115 926 3154
www.millcrofttextiles.co.uk
For a wide range of haberdashery and
bridal and occasion fabrics

VV Rouleaux
020 7730 3125
www.vvrouleaux.com
For a wide selection of beautiful
ribbons and trims

USA

Clotilde
800-545-4002
www.clotilde.com
For sewing supplies and advice

Connecting Threads
800-574-6454
www.connectingthreads.com
For general needlework supplies

Create For Less
1-866-333-4463
www.createforless.com
For a huge range of sewing and craft
supplies at discount prices

The Craft Connection
888-204-4050
www.craftconn.com
For fabrics and needlework supplies

Hancocks of Paducah
800-845-8723
www.hancocks-paducah.com
For general needlework supplies

JoAnn Stores Inc
888-739-4120
www.joann.com
For needlework and quilting supplies

M & J Trimming
800-965-8746
www.mjtrim.com
For a wide choice of trimmings and
accessories

✳ Index

appliqué 46

backstitch 36
bags
  on a chain 68–9, 90, 92
  chic holdall 28–31
  delicate gift 78–83
  embroidered shopping 36–9, 91
  holdall with scalloped edging
    40–1, 94
  linings 35, 39
  little 42–5
  shoulder 32–5, 88, 90
basket, pretty wicker 54–5, 91
beads, loops of 63
blanket stitch 15
bouquet, lace trim and ribbon 63
boxes, beautiful 84–7, 89, 92
broderie anglaise 19
brooch 71
button loops 49

candleholder, decorative 56–7, 90
chain handles 68–9

chair cover, pretty 16–19
charms 31, 40, 42, 71
clasps 77
cones, attractive 62–5, 89, 93
counterpane, patchwork 22–5
cushion, with star 6–9, 94
cushion pads 73

drawstring channels 56, 81

edgings
  broderie anglaise 19
  scalloped 40–1, 94
embroidery 36, 84, 91–2
  motif transfer 88

flaps 40
flounces 16, 19
flowers 20–1, 54, 56, 68–9
  embroidery 92
  patterns 89–92
  with pistils 65, 84
  pleated 28, 52–3, 90, 32

gift bags, delicate 78–83

handles 28, 31, 68–9
hanging loops 53
holdalls
  chic 28–31
  scalloped edged 40–1, 94

lavender pillows 73–5, 92
letters, embroidery 73, 92
linings
  bag 35, 39
  cone 65
  purse 77
long stitch 73

monograms 31, 40, 58, 78, 84

patchwork
  for bags 35, 36
  for counterpanes 22–5
patterns 88–95
photo frame, antique-style 14–15
pillow, lavender 73–5, 92

place setting 58–9, 88–9
pockets
  elasticated bag 35, 39
  integrated 49
  wallet 46, 49
pompoms, soft 60–1, 93
purse 76–7, 95

right-angles, cutting 11

screen, delicate 10–13
star cushion 6–9, 94
stitch types 15, 36, 73
stole 70–1
straps, shoulder 45

tablecloth with flowers 20–1, 90
ties 6, 16
trims 32, 42, 45, 58, 77, 84

wallet, pretty 46–9
wicker basket, pretty 54–5, 91
willow work 52–3, 90
wreath, decorative 52–3, 90